The only way you
are reading this, is if I am gone.

The only way you are reading this, is if I am gone.

Carrie Bolesky

Library of Congress Control Number:		2012903768
ISBN:	Hardcover	978-1-4691-7581-2
	Softcover	978-1-4691-7580-5
	Ebook	978-1-4691-7582-9

This book was printed in the United States of America.

To order additional copies of this book, contact:
Xlibris Corporation
1-888-795-4274
www.Xlibris.com
Orders@Xlibris.com

CONTENTS

Chapter 1   Tragedy...1

Chapter 2   Telling Our Family 5

Chapter 3   Andrea's Story 8

Chapter 4   The Hospital 12

Chapter 5   Back to Andrea...14

Chapter 6   The Funeral Home...20

Chapter 7   Tuesday, 5:00 p.m..24

Chapter 8   The Viewing 26

Chapter 9   Wednesday, 4:00 a.m...28

Chapter 10   The Funeral...30

Chapter 11   TJ's Funeral...31

Chapter 12   The Cemetery 32

Chapter 13   Thursday, 4:00 p.m. 33

Chapter 14   Jaw-Dropping News...36

Chapter 15   A New Journey Begins 41

Chapter 16   Dealing with Anger 46

Chapter 17   October 1, 2010 49

Chapter 18   Journey Through Grief...52

Chapter 19   Good versus Evil 54

Chapter 20   Not Right or Wrong—Just Different 56

Chapter 21   Dreams 59

Chapter 22   A Letter to TJ...62

Chapter 23   Hell 64

Chapter 24   Grandma Proctor...66

Chapter 25   End of 2011 68

Chapter 26   Wilsecks..69

Conclusion...73

Special Thank You...77

CHAPTER 1

TRAGEDY

WHEN MY SON TJ was nine years old, he announced at the dinner table one evening that as soon as he gets to heaven, he's going to ask God to sign his wing. Of course, this is the same child who, when asked how the family rooster got so mean all of a sudden, replied, "Maybe somebody tried to ride him!"

On September 12, 2010, at the age of sixteen years old, TJ had left our house with his friend Roy Wilseck and his girlfriend, Lydia (who was also Roy's younger sister), to attend a Sunday-night youth group meeting. Cassidy, our fifteen-year-old daughter, was going over to her boyfriend Colin's house after church to spend the afternoon with his family. Our thirteen-year-old daughter, Cami, wanted to have some quiet time at home by herself. Sounds like date night for my husband, Trent, and me!

We usually ride our bikes to a local restaurant downtown. When we arrived, I checked a missed call on my cell phone. The message from a friend said this, "There has been an accident with TJ, Roy, and Lydia… and I don't think TJ survived!!!"

Instantly my heart sank and began beating out of my chest! I relayed the message to Trent. Trent denied it immediately out of self-preservation. We started calling TJ's cell phone and texting as fast as we could. We then began texting TJ's friend Roy and TJ's girlfriend, Lydia. No answer! We were now panicked and rode our bikes back home. Our thoughts were racing, and it seemed like the longest mile-long ride ever.

"TJ! This is Mom! Please answer your phone!" The more I called his cell phone, the sicker I felt.

Trent thought, *Maybe this is a sick joke, or it could be mistaken identity or just wrong information!* He just knew this could not be true and felt we needed to get this cleared up before this gets around and people get hurt by this misinformation.

Myself… I knew. *There are no jokes like this. We had called everyone we knew, and no one was answering. Plus, most of the phones we called were turned off! What are the chances that dozens of people are all not answering?* The doubt in our minds began to really sink in, but we agreed not to react until we knew something for sure.

Once finally reaching home, we grabbed our daughter Cami and started driving the route they would have likely taken to get to church.

I remember feeling like I was going to throw up as we came upon the police cars, fire trucks, and ambulances, in a closed-up back-country road where we knew they would have been traveling. We tried to pull around the police cars, and they stopped us.

Trent said, "I think our son, TJ, was in this car accident… we need to see him!" They directed us to go around the blockade, and we could see the accident scene just a short way ahead. When we stopped the vehicle, we all jumped out and ran toward the accident, but once again, the police stopped us.

One officer asked us who we were, and we explained we were the parents of T. J. Bolesky, who we believed may have been in the accident. Trent began yelling at the top of his lungs, "TJ! TJ! TJ!"

The officer asked Trent for identification; and after Trent showed his driver's license, the officer, in a somber voice, said, "Yes, your son was in the accident… and I'm sorry. He didn't make it."

Trent fell to his knees and started sobbing! Cami and I instinctively reached for each other and began to cry out loud!

This could not be happening. This happened to other people, and I felt sorry for them and offered my words of encouragement. This doesn't happen to me! TJ was the centerpiece of our family! Our only son! I went into an emotional shock, where I would remain for months.

While still holding Cami, I asked the police if I could go say good-bye to my boy. I knew it would be bad, but I needed to kiss his bloodied face and give him to Jesus!

I understood when the police denied me. I am sure they do not want mothers to see their children in that condition. I wanted to see my son's wounds and thank God that he did not live through them. I needed to surrender him over to Jesus. I had been in the emergency room with all my kids over the years and had witnessed the accidents and blood associated with cuts that required stitching with no problems.

Later I found out that I couldn't see him because it would be tampering with a possible crime scene.

The officer told us he was being taken to the University of Michigan hospital and that we could see him there at the site.

CHAPTER 2

TELLING OUR FAMILY

ON OUR WAY to the hospital, the three of us began to make the dreaded calls to family. We called our daughter Cassidy, who was at her boyfriend's, to meet us at the hospital. We did not tell her about TJ's demise right away. Her boyfriend, Colin, and his parents, John and Nancy Slaughter, started to bring Cassidy and Colin to the hospital to join us.

Next I called my mom.

"MOM!" I cried. "TJ WAS IN A CAR ACCIDENT AND DIED!"

TJ and Roy had just spent the weekend up north with my mom and stepdad, Russ, helping to put a new roof on their cabin. She had just seen him the day before. Something seems to tell you that if you've just seen that person, there is no way they could die in that short time frame.

Mom said calmly, "No, Carrie... no."

Her voice sounded like she was deep in thought. "Honey... you're probably confused and may have gotten the wrong information. We'll come and help you get this straightened out."

I persisted, "Mom… Roy, Lydia, and TJ were in a car accident, and TJ is *dead*!"

She replied, "No… no… Carrie… are you saying TJ is dead?"

I began sobbing and said, "Yes, Mom! We are leaving the accident scene and on our way to the hospital!" My mom recalled later that she fell to her knees, laid her head on Russ's lap, and sobbed.

They started off to the hospital but still really did *not* believe that TJ could be gone. *He must just be in critical condition,* they thought.

I was sobbing uncontrollably now and called my dad. He recounts getting my call around 6:00 p.m., about an hour after the accident occurred. I usually did not call them on a Sunday evening, so immediately he wondered why I would be calling. When he picked up the phone and heard me crying, he instantly knew something had happened to one of the kids. He said that he and my stepmom, Betty, would be on the way to the hospital right away. Dad said that after he hung up the phone, he dropped to his knees and sobbed. He and Betty hugged and cried and then headed for the hospital.

It was especially heartbreaking in another way for my husband, Trent. Trent had lost a brother in a family tragedy twenty-five years earlier, so his parents had been through this with losing their own son, Hal. Upon receiving the news, Trent's mom, Marilyn, was understandably hysterical as she was instantly reliving an all-too-familiar nightmare.

Trent's family lives in Florida, and we live in Michigan. Trent's mom called her daughter, Stacy, who lives a few miles from her. But Mom could not get all the words to come out, so it took Stacy a few minutes to try to understand what Marilyn was trying to say.

Trent called his dad, Tracy, and stepmom, Jeannie. Trent said to his dad, "Dad… I don't know how you got through this when Hal died, and I don't know how I'll get through this either!"

Word spread throughout our family in Florida, and airlines were being called and preparations made for immediate departures. Word spread to Trent's family in Aruba, Texas, Ohio, Pennsylvania, Indiana, South Carolina, and California.

Our family started popping up on prayer chains everywhere. Trent and I come from a Christian heritage, and the churches of our aunts, uncles, cousins, and extended families were called to put us into their immediate prayer chain. I don't know how many people were praying for us that night; but it had to be hundreds, if not thousands, of people praying for us.

CHAPTER 3

ANDREA'S STORY

I ASKED ANDREA Wilseck, Roy and Lydia's mother, to write on her experiences that night, September 12, 2010.

I would like to introduce her first and then follow with her story.

Andrea was TJ's teacher in the Christian school he attended in the 2009 through 2010 school year. It was a small school, and the high school students were in one large room.

That year, Trent and I had decided to put TJ and Cassidy in that school. Cami, our youngest daughter, had been doing well in public school.

Andrea homeschooled her youngest, Josiah, who was fourteen, and Lydia, fifteen. So they would come to school with Andrea every day to just do their work there.

TJ and Josiah became friends quickly. They constantly harassed each other and joked around most of their day every day.

The Wilsecks lived about an hour from the school, so sometimes

TJ would go home with them on the weekends to be with Josiah and come back on Mondays to school with them.

The following is Andrea's story:

I LOOKED AT the clock. It was four thirty. Josiah, our thirteen-year-old, had turned off the Detroit Lions on TV since it was the "worst game ever." The phone rang. I heard our seventeen-year-old son, Roy, say, "Mom, I got in an accident. I think I hit something, and TJ's arm…" I couldn't really understand what he was saying.

Once Roy told me where he was, I dropped the phone, called Josiah, and told him, "Roy has been in an accident. He said something about TJ's arm. I think it might be broken. I'm going to get them. Call 911 and report an accident on Curtis and Six Mile." As I drove, I called my husband, Tim. I told him that the kids had been in an accident, but I didn't think it was a big deal.

Once I reached Six Mile, the road was blocked off, and there were fire trucks and police cars all down the road. A police officer told me I could not go down there, but I told him my kids were down there. He moved aside, and I drove as far down as I could. As I got closer, I saw Roy standing on the side of the road; he was standing by some lady, and his jeep was in the ditch completely smashed. I put the van in park and ran out to be with Roy. As I passed my fifteen-year-old daughter, Lydia, in the middle of the road, I saw a group of firefighters around her. I ran to Roy and hugged him. He grabbed me and said, "Mom, I don't know where TJ is."

I turned to the lady who was standing there. "There were three kids in that jeep!"

"I know" was all she said.

"No, you don't understand, there was another kid in the jeep. Where's TJ? We have to find him!"

She didn't say anything at first, and then she quietly said, "We know where he is."

"Where, where is TJ?" I pleaded with her.

She leaned in close to my ear so Roy wouldn't hear and said, "He didn't make it."

I felt as if someone had sucked all the air out of me. I could not believe what I had just heard. I screamed out, "Oh God, oh God…" and I grabbed Roy. He was crying and screaming too. We stood there and held each other, crying and screaming. How could this be? It had to be a mistake. As we stood there, Tim came up from the other side. He walked up to us and put his arms around us both, and we all cried. Time stood still as the three of us stood in the middle of the road, holding each other.

A paramedic came up to us and brought us quickly back to reality. He said that he needed to take Roy over to the ambulance to be checked out. As we all turned to go to the ambulance, another paramedic came over to Tim and me.

"We are going to have your daughter airlifted to Mott's Children's Hospital at U of M," he told us.

"But," I started, "our insurance is with the Saint John system."

"No, you *want* her to go to U of M," he insistently stated.

It was at that point that I looked back toward Lydia. There were four or five people surrounding her, but she was not moving. I guess I knew she was hurt badly. After all, she *was* thrown out of the jeep.

I agreed that they should send Lydia to Mott's. My thoughts turned to Josiah. We needed to get him, and there were people to call. TJ's parents needed to be called! I turned to Tim. "I have to call Carrie."

A police officer overheard me and interrupted, "That is not your job. That is our job. We are trained for situations like this. You need to be there for your children. You are not to call his parents."

I nodded, and I trusted that the police would contact them soon and would do a better job than I could at that moment.

The police then told me that I should ride in the ambulance with Roy and that Tim should get Josiah and meet us there. A friend from church was a member of the volunteer firefighters, and he offered to drive Tim to the hospital.

I jumped in the front of the ambulance and looked out the windshield. I could see the paramedics putting Lydia on a backboard. She looked so small.

There was a couple on a motorcycle that had witnessed the accident. The driver was talking to the police, but his passenger, a woman, was still sitting on the bike. She looked up at me and mouthed the words, "I'm sorry."

"I'm sorry." The words tore me up. "I'm sorry." That's what people say when they don't know what to say when someone dies. Someone did die. TJ died. My head started spinning, and the tears ran down my cheeks. I could not stop them. I stopped worrying about Roy and Lydia and just sat there crying for TJ. How can a sixteen-year-old boy, so young, die?

CHAPTER 4

THE HOSPITAL

WHEN WE ARRIVED at the ER, we were met by TJ's principal and her husband, who had been called to help the Wilsecks since their children were there at the hospital with serious injuries. Roy had only minor injuries, but Lydia would be a different story.

We were ushered into a family waiting room as friends and family began to appear. My parents, pastors, Colin's family, and other close family gathered around us. Liz, my sister, and her husband, Thomas, had the farthest to come. Liz had always been close to my kids, especially TJ, who loved to wrestle with her younger boys. Liz had to pick herself off the floor after getting the call as well.

We all took turns crying, telling funny stories about TJ, crying again, and praying. It all kept cycling. My dad assured me that we would make it through this.

My mother, Debbie, and Liz became my personal spokespeople to the hospital staff. They hurried themselves around the hospital to find someone to let me see my son. They were not getting any answers. They seemed to be brushed off from one person to the next.

A mother deals with a lot of blood and other unsightly things, especially with boys. I just wanted to see him.

As a mother, you worry about your kid's safety. You want to give them pain medicine or Band-Aids or a sucker to make them feel better. I knew I wouldn't need any of these to make TJ feel better. I wouldn't be able to fix him this time. I still wanted to hold his limp, broken body and assess the damage. I wanted proof that he would not wake up in a dark, cold morgue alone and scared.

We had learned that TJ's girlfriend, Lydia, had been clinging to life and had been airlifted to the hospital. Later we found out from the rescue team that no one thought that she would live to make it to the hospital. At the scene, it looked grim. They said that even if she did survive, she would have extensive brain damage.

I was never allowed to say good-bye to my son that night. The hospital's family advocate finally told us that TJ had to be seen by the medical examiner and then sent to the funeral home. We were all going home that night knowing there was nothing else we could do to see him.

I was devastated.

CHAPTER 5

BACK TO ANDREA

THE AMBULANCE PULLED into the hospital. Roy was taken down a hall while the paramedic led me to the waiting room. No one knew what was happening to Lydia. They thought she had been taken into surgery.

Just before we walked in, my phone started to vibrate: TJ's Mom-Carrie Bolesky, the display read. "Tim, TJ's mom is calling me." I wanted to answer it, but Tim reminded me that I should not be the one to deliver this news to her. I ignored the call, and it was the hardest thing I had to do.

Tim and Josiah got there, and we were led into Roy's room. He was sitting up in the hospital bed, and a nurse was getting some glass out of his arm. Roy seemed okay. He asked about Lydia, but he seemed disconnected. Did he even hear about TJ at the scene?

There was a knock at the door, and a police officer entered.

"Roy," he addressed my son, "I'd like to ask you a few questions."

Roy agreed, and the officer asked him what had happened. Roy said he didn't actually remember.

"We were driving home from TJ's house, and Lydia and TJ were teasing me because I had gotten a text from this girl I like. I got distracted, and

I moved over the center yellow line. I turned the wheel too much in the opposite direction, and then I was in the ditch."

He wasn't upset; he just told it straight out. I walked out of the room as my phone was going off again. I had missed two calls from Carrie and a few texts. My heart was breaking for this mother who could not find her son. I could not understand why the police would not have informed them yet!

Tim and I decided that we had to tell Roy about TJ. "Roy," Tim began, "Roy, TJ didn't make it."

Roy did not move. He sat there and cried silently. Tears streamed down his cheeks. I asked him if he already knew that TJ was gone. He shook his head no. Looking back, I think part of him might have known because he never asked about TJ, only about Lydia.

"Roy," Tim began again, "whatever you are feeling right now is perfectly fine. If you want to scream, you can. If you want to cry, it's okay. Whatever you're feeling is perfectly okay."

We all sat there quietly. I held Roy's hand, and my heart broke for my son. Roy had always wanted a best friend. Most of Roy's close friends had different priorities than Roy, and they would end up drifting apart. TJ, like Roy, had the same family background. They had grown close quickly, and I thought he finally found the best friend he had always been looking for.

A nurse interrupted us to tell us that the Boleskys were on their way to the hospital, and they wanted to see Roy.

Carrie and Trent were on their way here?

What would the Boleskys say to Roy? They had every right to be angry at Roy, every right to know exactly what had happened, every right to hate right now, every right.

I walked out of Roy's room and turned the corner. There was Carrie. She grabbed me, and we balled and cried and held each other as though our very lives depended on us just holding each other. Then she spoke into my ear, "We both lost a son tonight because you loved TJ as if he was your own."

I did not know what to say. She was graciously giving me the okay to grieve for a boy I loved. She was allowing me to be okay with my grief, to release my guilt over feeling an incredible loss, even when my kids were still alive. It was overwhelming; I excused myself and returned to Roy's room.

Tim turned to Roy. "You don't have to see anyone if you don't want to or if you're not ready."

"I want to see them," Roy stated. My son, my little boy, looked so grown-up to me right then. There is always an accident every year involving young people. You hear about them all the time. Sometimes alcohol is a factor, or speed. But not this time. And these things happen to other people's children, not mine. In fact, I had just told the kids about the accident that happened when I was in high school. Three boys—all popular football players—were driving to school and passed a school bus on a hill. They were hit by an oncoming car, and only the driver lived. I told the kids because I wanted them to be super careful driving and to know that you have another's life in your hands. TJ had stated that he could never forgive himself if he had been that driver. And now that driver was my own son!

The nurse gave Roy a shirt to put on, and we walked out of his room. I was very fearful. The three of us, Tim, Roy, and myself, entered into a small waiting room. Trent and Carrie were there. Trent hugged Roy, and then Carrie hugged Roy. Trent looked Roy in the eye and said, "Roy, this is not your fault."

I stood there not believing what I had just heard. He didn't say, "What happened? What did you do? You killed my son."

No. He said, "Roy this is not your fault."

He continued, "We serve a God who does not make accidents. This was TJ's time to go, and nothing you could have done would have stopped that. We believe that all the days of TJ's life were written before he ever came to be, and if he hadn't died with you in that jeep, he would have died some other way tonight. TJ would hate it if you blame yourself."

I knew that I had just witnessed true faith, a faith that stands on God's Word when life doesn't make sense, a faith that loves others and shows kindness, a faith that I was lacking with all my piles of "whys."

Carrie echoed what Trent had said and again told Roy that TJ would be so sad if Roy would blame himself. We all hugged and said how incredibly sorry we were. Carrie held me and again said to me, "You lost a son too tonight. I know you loved my boy as though he was your own." I have never felt such love. This mom, this incredible mom, was including me in her grief, giving me permission to mourn. I sobbed. I did love TJ as though he was my own, and I thought no one was going to understand why my grief was so strong, but here was his mom telling me she understood.

After meeting with Carrie and Trent, the five of us walked out of the waiting room. We saw TJ's family gathered together in a larger waiting room. One by one, they came out of the waiting room and confronted Roy.

First was TJ's grandma Townley, Carrie's mom, who had just had both TJ and Roy up at her cabin the day before. She hugged Roy and said, "Roy, you are a great guy, and this isn't your fault."

Then TJ's grandpa Carpenter, Carrie's dad, said, "Roy," and he shook Roy's hand. "I'm TJ's grandfather. I'm sorry."

Each one of TJ's relatives, probably about twenty, came out, and the same scene was played out over and over. Some knew Roy and stated how great he was, and some were just meeting him for the first time. Each one echoed the statement that God does not make mistakes; this was not Roy's fault.

Our family was lining the walls, watching this outpouring of love, grace, and acceptance happening right in front of us. None of us said anything.

The Boleskys began to leave, but not before they asked about Lydia and promised to pray for us all. Tim and I sought out a nurse who filled us in on Lydia's status.

The nurse took Tim and me to the ICU to see her. She was medically sedated and had her own nurse stationed at the foot of her bed. She looked so small and had many tubes inserted in her. We were able to see her, touch her, and kiss her.

Lydia was connected to multiple tubes, and there was a mini nurse's station at the foot of her bed. She was under constant care. She looked so small. Was she able to breathe on her own? Her nurse said that everything looked good.

That night, Tim and I and the boys spent the first of many nights in what we eventually referred to as hospital city.

The doctors had determined that she had a broken bone in her elbow, a shattered knee, and multiple internal injuries. They took her into surgery and cleaned all the injuries. They removed the shattered kneecap, leaving her with about one fourth of her original kneecap. Her elbow was not broken, just had a large gash. Internally, her liver and spleen had received some sort of damage. Her clavicle bone in her left shoulder was broken. She also had multiple cuts and looked like what you would imagine someone to look like when thrown out of a moving vehicle.

I got up and walked into her room.

She was heavily sedated and very still. I watched the machines work for her, sustaining her life. How could this have happened? As I looked at Lydia, lying there bruised and broken, guilt settled in. Here was my daughter, my little girl, and next to her in ICU was an empty bed. A bed where TJ should have been lying. I dreaded telling her.

Then I felt the vibration of my cell again. The display read, TJ's Mom-Carrie Bolesky. I moved through everyone to be alone. When I read the message, I fell to my knees. "Lord," I cried out, "how can anyone one have this much faith?" Carrie was again showing me real, true faith. Here she was, not even twenty-four hours since her son was taken from her, sending me encouragement.

Dear Andrea, I love you.
Thank you for loving my son like your very own.
He would be sad that he is the source of our broken hearts.
Soon we will be able to celebrate his life.

We stood by Lydia's bed, and the doctor pulled up her multiple scans on the computer. Lydia's brain had actually bruised itself by smashing against her skull. We would not know the extent of the damage until she was brought out of sedation. She had a broken clavicle and multiple bruises to her upper body. The doctor said that it would be best to take her into surgery to repair her clavicle.

Internally, her spleen and liver had received damage. Head trauma, internal organ damage, and more surgery?

I felt the vibration of my phone in my pocket; the display read, TJ's Mom-Carrie Bolesky. I excused myself and left the room. I had made a vow that no matter what, I would always take Carrie's calls.

Carrie was calling to ask if we would be willing to talk to the news. She told me that they had been interviewed by channel 4. I was so upset for them. How dare they disturb this wonderful family at this time!

"Carrie, I'm so sorry that they are contacting you."

But Carrie sounded great. She was calm, at peace. "No," she said, "we are glad to be interviewed. We get to tell TJ's story and how God has been such a part of it." I was again blown away by this faith.

CHAPTER 6

THE FUNERAL HOME

SEPTEMBER 12 WAS the worst day of our lives. That night we drove home from the hospital about midnight. Trent and I sat with our daughters in the living room. We sat there in silence, absorbing the shock. We were devastated. We were clueless as to what to do.

The next few hours and days are still a blur to me. I remember family in and out of the house, doing things for us that we couldn't do. My mom and sister put together the pictures to take to the funeral while Trent and I went to Boric Jennings's funeral home to make arrangements.

I had to leave the room at the funeral home several times to break down. I got home and went directly to the bathroom to throw up while my mom held my hair.

I remember continuously shaking like I had had about ten cups of coffee. I sat and stared, intermittently crying while everyone helped with plans.

It was Tuesday, two days after TJ died. We received the call from the Boric Jennings that TJ was ready for viewing. I had been terribly upset that I hadn't been able to see him at the accident site or the hospital on Sunday night or Monday.

I asked to be alone with TJ first. The door closed behind me, and I started toward the casket. I saw the back of his head first. I sobbed uncontrollably, shocked that that was my little cowboy (as I still jokingly called him even though he was sixteen) lying here in a casket.

That is *TJ!* I thought. *And he's really dead.* I let the mortified devastation overwhelm me, knowing somehow that it was necessary for healing.

Wow. I never thought in all my life that I would be standing here looking at my only son in a casket.

My dating, marriage, early motherhood, and dreams of my future flashed through my mind. This was never part of it. I couldn't wrap my mind around what was happening to us. It felt like a nightmare, but I knew it was real. I just was instinctively taking one hour at a time because I knew that was my only choice. How would I live through this? Was I going to be committed to a mental institution after I got through this first week of numbness and shock? I had no idea.

My mind went back to his birth. I nursed him until he was a year old. We were so attached. I couldn't leave him in the church nursery until he was three because he had such bad separation anxiety. I remembered his first day of school, which wasn't until he was in second grade because I had homeschooled him until then.

I was so sick with chronic fatigue syndrome when he was between five years old and nine years old. I fell asleep at the drop of a hat and felt like I was running a high fever for those four years. TJ obeyed my instructions and was responsible for Cassie and Cami during that time. I depended on him, and he was so loyal to me.

In the past year, TJ grew to five feet eleven inches and bent down to hug me all the time. He was responsible, sensitive to me, and honored me. We were closer than I ever imagined I would be to my son at his age. And yet he was even closer to his dad!

How he could be lying in this casket at sixteen years old! He was tall, was thin, had the ideal girlfriend, and had a 1988 Camaro. I threw myself on his cold, hard body and sobbed. I slipped my hand over his hair. Yes, that was his hairline all right.

No, TJ! Please come back, I inwardly pleaded! *Don't go. I will throw my life away for you! God, please take me and not him!* But it was too late for bargaining.

I inspected his body. They did well to hide his injuries. I found where his neck and wrists had been broken. I found the sewed up cut on his head where the impact had been. I felt his middle where his ribs had been crushed from both sides. I looked for all his wounds. I knew his head was damaged because of his fatal hit to the tree. I didn't get to assess him after the accident, so this was important to me. It helped me heal to know that his injuries caused him to die instantly, with no pain.

I slipped my hand under his cold, rubbery one. Tears streaming down my cheeks, I whispered, "I'm sorry, TJ, that your body was so hurt and broken that I could not fix it this time."

"Remember when you stabbed your hand with a knife, and you didn't tell me for an hour because you didn't want me to know how dumb you were?" A smile broke through my tears. "We made the hospital staff laugh at all our jokes while they were stitching you up! The same happened when you stabbed your thumb with an EpiPen."

My heart sank into the pit of my stomach. The overwhelming sorrow felt like it was too much to bear, and I fell on him and cried. My heart physically ached.

I couldn't process how he could be hurt so badly that he died. This time the injuries had been so bad that he ceased living. That's never happened to us before.

Liz and Cami came in, and we all cried together. I showed them his injuries. We all combed through his hair and body like monkeys do to each other. It reminded me of an animal show I saw where a baby monkey was snatched by an alligator and the mom rescued it, but it had already died. The mom held it in her arms as the other monkeys came to assess the damage all over its body.

Chapter 7

TUESDAY, 5:00 P.M.

WHILE I WAS up at the computers trying to tell everyone about how this was all a blessing, the news report played on televisions all over the metro area. One television in one waiting room of the hospital was being watched by my family and by Roy. I walked into the waiting room after the broadcast was over to find Roy extremely upset. He came over to me with tears in his eyes, and I held him.

From what I could understand from Roy, the interview with Carrie and Trent was powerful. They had strongly proclaimed that they believed in a God who doesn't make mistakes. They would miss TJ every day, but they knew God was in control. But then, the reporter went on to say that charges may be brought against Roy for vehicular manslaughter. Roy was beside himself. Wasn't it enough that his best friend had died and that his sister was in ICU?

TJ and Roy spent all summer together. Usually you could find them driving, top off, in Roy's jeep heading to the lake. One weekend, TJ, Roy, and Josiah decided they would go out into the woods to have a "man" weekend. They were going to sleep out, cook out, cut themselves, walk through fire—do man stuff. They went to the house of TJ's grandma and set up camp out on her property. As night came, they walked over to her house looking for a flashlight. They were trying to get back to their campsite but got lost. They ended up in TJ's car, where they decided they would sleep until it became light, and then they could get back to their tent.

After a short time of trying to sleep, they then decided that they should just drive back to TJ's house and maybe grab a pizza on their way home, except that none of them were fully dressed. So Josiah, in Roy's shirt, his own boxers, and TJ's shoes, walked in to get the pizza.

Once back at TJ's house, they decided to spend the rest of the weekend watching movies, going bowling, and having Mr. Bolesky grill steaks for them. None of them could contact Lydia, or they would have ended up telling her how they wimped out of their "man" weekend.

And now they wanted to charge Roy with TJ's death? This was too much. I tried to assure Roy that God was still in control, but this faith, a Bolesky kind of faith, was new to me. Could God allow, or even want, this? What good would come out of Roy being put in jail?

CHAPTER 8

THE VIEWING

WEDNESDAY WAS THE viewing. The line to see us and TJ was outside the funeral home door. We were overwhelmed by the love people had for us and for TJ. We had so much peace with the number of people there to help us and support us as much as they could.

I was so appreciative of people coming from our bank, our video store, our doctor's offices, and Mr. B's restaurant, which we frequently visited. It was community coming together for us.

With all our family in from all over the country, people from our church, my parents' churches, and friends from previous places we had lived, the funeral home was overflowing with love and compassion.

Our family of now four hung on a balance of prayer from this group, and we bathed in their warmth. We relied on their strength. We had no other choice for survival.

It was a long, exhausting day. I appreciated people just saying, "I'm sorry." That's all one needs to say. That's all one needs to hear.

CHAPTER 9

WEDNESDAY, 4:00 A.M.

I WAS AWAKE again, back at the scene. I saw it clearly again: running to Roy, holding him, our screams crying out together.

Again, reality was in the ICU waiting room.

I had no idea what to expect from the visitation today. The memory of the Boleskys and the faith they showed to us and Roy was strong in my mind, but I didn't know if they would still feel the same when they saw us all today at TJ's visitation. And even if they could still show love to us, what about everyone else that might show up? What if someone said something hurtful to Roy? What if more reporters were there?

I began to have doubts. I needed to see that newscast from last night. I needed to hear Carrie and Trent's interview.

I went up to the hospital computers and searched for their interview.

The only report I could find on the web brought me nothing but anger and confusion. The reporter stated that Roy had been distracted by Lydia. He made the disheartening statement, "charges may be brought against the driver."

The interview with Carrie and Trent was nowhere to be found. I searched all the sites I could find. No Carrie, no Trent, no God, no faith statement, no salvation message—nothing positive.

Tim came with the boys. I got dressed, and we did the hardest thing we had to do: leave Lydia. The drive to the funeral home was a long quiet drive. No one really talked. Tim drove very slowly and made sure he did not crowd other drivers. None of us had discussed it, but we were all concerned about how Roy would react to certain situations. Any family member that drove with Roy drove extremely carefully, and no one drove past the accident site.

I realized that our kids have never been at a funeral. I started to tell Roy and the boys what would happen today at the visitation and tomorrow at the funeral. We told Roy we were there for him and whatever he needed, we would make happen.

We slowly made our way into the funeral home. Trent came right up to us and hugged us all. The very first thing he said to us was that he had heard the newscasts and the possibility of pressing charges. He told us that he personally called the sheriff to tell him that that would be unnecessary. What a blessing to hear that from Trent!

Then Carrie came over and hugged us all. She welcomed us as if we were family. She walked us to the casket. She told me I should stand beside her 'cause I loved TJ like a son. Cassie and Cami, TJ's sisters, came over to us and hugged us. The family asked Roy to stay for lunch with the family. Such grace! These were the true Christians. These were the salt and light of Christ's love.

CHAPTER 10

THE FUNERAL

THE FUNERAL ON Thursday, September 16, was nice. There were over four hundred people in attendance. Trent did the funeral and did a great job telling funny stories about TJ and also on how we knew that he was in heaven. My cousin Betsy sang "Legacy" by Natalie Grant.

We had photos of TJ set to Phil Collins's song "You'll Be in My Heart." The story behind that is this:

My brother Andy and TJ were very close. Andy lives in Florida and came up for a visit when TJ was about seven years old. TJ was so sad when Andy had to go back home.

We had a CD from the cartoon *Tarzan* in the car. TJ kept replaying Phil Collins's song "You'll Be in My Heart" when he thought about Uncle Andy leaving as tears streamed down his little face. That so breaks a mama's heart, but there's nothing I could do but let him cry it out.

Nobody at the funeral outside our family knew the story behind us picking that song, but it was emotional either way.

Chapter 11

TJ'S FUNERAL

I HAD TO go home from the hospital to get ready. I left Lydia and returned to our house. I had not been home since Sunday, when the accident happened. It was the most depressing place now. It was so empty and quiet here without TJ. Would it ever be the same again?

Carrie had asked Roy and Joe to be pallbearers. As we entered into the church, Tim took the boys to the front and stayed with them. It was so hard to be there, to hear the words, to realize that TJ was gone and not coming back. It was healing also, though.

We sang "Blessed Be His Name." The words will forever have tremendous meaning to me:

He gives and takes away, but my heart will choose to say, Blessed be His Name.

CHAPTER 12

THE CEMETERY

THE GRAVESIDE SERVICE was brief, which was good. I was emotionally exhausted. Boric Jennings had been such a good funeral home. They made things as easy as possible and worked with us so sensitively. At the end of the graveside service, they released a dove to signify letting TJ's spirit go to heaven. TJ would have loved the fact that the dove pooped when released!

Then, large drops of rain began to fall quickly. Once everyone had gotten into their cars, the sky released the biggest downpour I had seen in a long time. I thanked God for holding the waters back until the end and also for letting me know that he was crying with me.

To this day, whenever we have a big rainstorm, it triggers grieving in my soul, and I cry. It tends to wash through me, and then I am comforted by God.

Blessed be those who mourn, for they will be comforted. (Matthew 5:4)

Chapter 13

THURSDAY, 4:00 P.M.

ONCE WE RETURNED to the hospital, Lydia's breathing tube was out and she was asking for us. We went in to see her, and in a matter of seconds, she was asking for TJ. She needed to know; not knowing would not help her healing. Tim told her, and she cried. She said he couldn't be dead because he had visited her in the hospital. I want to believe he did. I want to believe he came up to her bed and said, "Hello, little girl" in his little voice, like he used to.

She was so sad. She said he was perfect, and she would never find anyone like him again. She was where we all had been on Sunday—in disbelief. She slept and woke, cried and talked a little. She asked to call his phone, to hear his voice again.

The saddest thing she said was that TJ once told her if he ever died, she would die with him. I told her that was TJ's plan, not God's. But how could she get her mind around that? She had missed all the God moments. She missed seeing the love that the Boleskys were pouring out on us, on Roy. She missed the visitation and the funeral. And she missed TJ; she would always miss TJ.

SUMMER 2010—TWO MONTHS BEFORE THE ACCIDENT.

I was thinking about this summer, TJ's last summer.

Lydia and Josiah were planning on going to Washtenaw Technical Middle School (WTMC) in September. WTMC is a high school located on the campus of Washtenaw Community College.

I encouraged TJ to apply, and he eventually did.

One night in July, TJ was over, and he got a call from his dad. He had just gotten his letter; he had been accepted into WTMC for the fall! He would be with Lydia for school again!

That was our last night home before we were to leave with the youth group for a mission trip to Jamaica. I told TJ that he had to leave early to go home as we needed to finish packing and get some sleep.

About half hour after he left, my cell phone rang, and it was TJ.

"Lydia," I said, "it's TJ."

"Then answer it," she said.

I was a little worried. Just a week before, Ahna had her boyfriend over, and he left very late. On his way home, he had gotten tired and drove off the road. When my phone started to ring from TJ, all I could think was, he got into a car accident.

"Hello," I answered the phone.

"Wilseck," TJ jumped right into what he wanted to say. "You know how you're always saying that this summer is going to be the best summer ever?"

"Yeah," I said.

"Well, I think you're right. I have a car [always the car was first], a girlfriend, two families that care about me, and I just got into the best school for next year."

"Yup," I said, "best summer ever. Now do you want to talk to Lydia?"

I handed the phone over to Lydia. This really was going to be the best summer ever.

All summer, TJ was over, or Lydia was with him. They were able to go up north to his family's cabin in June and to Ohio in July. They spent several weeks hanging out with his family, fishing, and going to Cedar Point. In August, TJ went with us to Orlando, Florida.

END OF HOSPITAL CITY

Lydia made great progress. She was moved to a rehab unit right after the funeral. She began physical therapy and began to heal physically. Emotionally, she asked few questions, which I told her I would always answer truthfully.

There were many discussions on what would need to be done in order to bring her home. We would need a ramp, possibly, since she would more than likely be in a wheelchair. We discussed having to put a shower and a hospital bed in our first floor; we also discussed putting in an elevating chair lift for our stairs. All these discussions were a waste of time since Lydia, beyond anyone's imagination, walked out of the hospital the following Monday, one week and one day after the accident, on crutches. She had a miraculous physical healing.

CHAPTER 14

JAW-DROPPING NEWS

IT HAS BEEN two weeks since TJ died. Our youngest daughter, Cami, has been cleaning and organizing TJ's room just the way he would have liked to have it done. He was a neat and clean young man.

His room has become a kind of a shrine to all things TJ and a place we could unite and grieve in the evenings to soft music and candlelight, crying and praying together.

Cami was organizing his closet and began to stare at the top shelf. She noticed a globe in the back top corner of his closet. She also noticed that the countries did not line up properly.

It appeared as though the globe was in two halves and that it had come apart, and TJ had inadvertently put the two halves back together improperly. The top half of the globe was uneven with the bottom half of the globe.

Cami got it down to put it in order; however, when she picked it up, she realized something was moving around inside the globe.

She shook it, and it appeared to be hollow inside the globe. But what could be inside? She took it apart.

When she opened it, she made a shocking discovery. She began yelling at the top of her lungs frantically. Trent, Cassie, and I were downstairs in the living room when we heard her distressed calling.

I thought, *Oh no! Now what?* We took off running upstairs and burst into TJ's room. Cami appeared to be in shock, sitting on TJ's bed and sobbing uncontrollably.

"Look! Look!" she exclaimed.

TJ had made the globe into a time capsule of his life. He had put his favorite *Pokémon* cards from his youth, a number of shark's teeth from his fishing adventures to the Florida Keys with his grandpa and grandma Bolesky, the ticket to his first middle school dance where he had his first slow dance with a girl, a bucket list of things he wanted to do before he died, and many other memorabilia.

More incredibly, he had put together a photo album documenting his life in a chronological manner, beginning with the first minutes of his life. There were pictures of him as a baby, then as a toddler, with his favorite family members, with his pets, and with friends he loved. We looked at each picture in amazement but had no idea what was to come next—the real shock!

When we came to the last page of the photo album, we saw that he had handwritten a note to his family on the back inside cover.

It read as follows:

The only way you have just seen these photos, is if I'm gone. Remember me as I was, on a good day. ☺ Do

not miss me, because I am in heaven with God. We
are probably having quite a good time.

I love everyone

Love, TJ Bolesky

We felt suspended in an animated state of amazement and awe.
We were all crying and holding each other. This horrible roller-
coaster ride of emotions we were on these first two weeks after his
death had just taken another odd turn, and all we could do was
hang on for the wild ride. This has made us miss him even more,
knowing he had been looking out for us. Oddly, somehow, God
allowed TJ to know that he would not be long for this world and let
him leave for us this gift—the globe!

These events triggered Trent's memory of having a conversation
with TJ about heaven.

Trent and TJ were sitting on the back patio swing, watching the
sunset together as they did on most summer nights.

TJ was asking a series of questions about heaven and what
people do there. Trent asked TJ why he was so deep in thought
about heaven and the afterlife.

That is when TJ declared, "Dad, I just know I am going there
soon! I am not kidding, Dad, I know I am going to die young!"

Trent says that as they talked about it, they both got emotional
and teary eyed. Then Trent reassured TJ that it is good for everyone to
wonder about these things from time to time. Then Trent dismissed
the thought of TJ dying from his own mind, not really wanting to
go there ever again.

Who could have imagined that TJ was accurate in his visions and thoughts? What had he been shown, and how had he known?

TJ's Bucket List

1. Be in a bike marathon
2. Own three dogs
3. Stay married to one person
4. Ride the Millennium Force (a ride at Cedar Point)
5. Go to Michigan State University
6. Don't drop out of high school
7. Go out of the country
8. Read the Bible cover to cover
9. Go to Alaska
10. Hunt a black bear
11. Save a life
12. Go whale watching
13. Get a job at a zoo
14. Go to an Atlantic Falcons game
15. Catch a foul baseball
16. Go scuba diving
17. Go to Africa
18. Eat a whole pizza by myself
19. Catch a wild alligator

TJ did accomplish numbers 11, 15, and 18. He pulled Cassidy out of a rip current in Lake Erie one time when she was drowning. We believe that TJ saved Lydia's life in the accident. He had his arm around her and took the hit from the tree on one side and from

Lydia on the other. We thought about doing the things on TJ's bucket list, as a family, but no one has stepped up to number 19. Let me know if you want to take one for the team. ☺

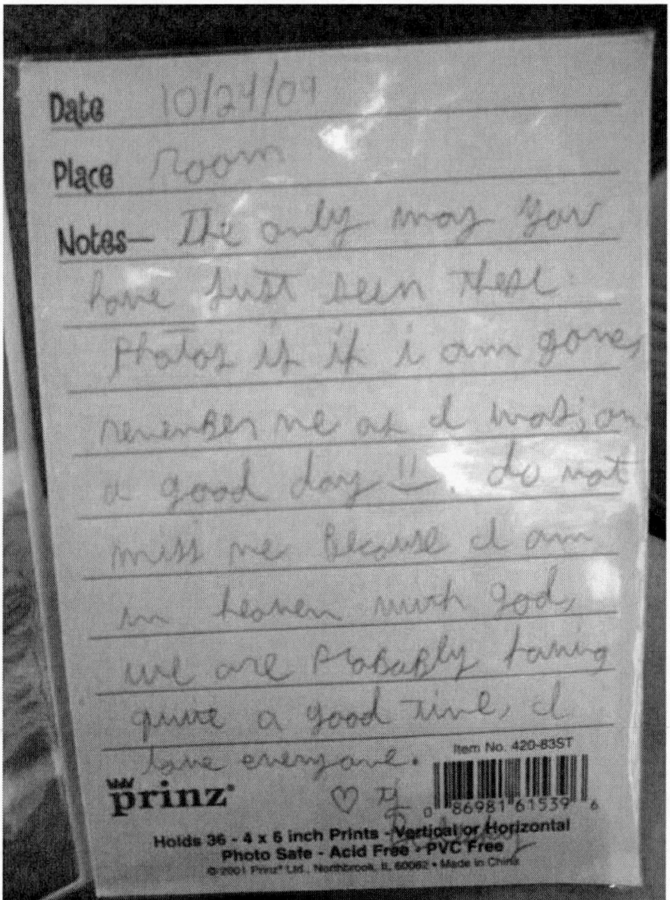
Date 10/24/07
Place Room
Notes— The only way you have just seen these photos is if i am gone, remember me as I was on a good day!! do not miss me because I am in heaven with god, we are probably having quite a good time, I love everyone.
Item No. 420-83ST
prinz
Holds 36 - 4 x 6 inch Prints - Vertical or Horizontal
Photo Safe - Acid Free - PVC Free

CHAPTER 15

A NEW JOURNEY BEGINS

I WROTE A journal for the next year to try to make sense of my new circumstances. The following passages are my journal entries:

I am reading everything I can get my hands on. I've read every book on grieving that has been given to me. They've been helpful. I'm new at this and know this could affect my family for better or worse. I can't lose another family member emotionally, so I'm taking to heart all advice being offered.

Losing someone who is so close to you, as TJ was to our family, causes you to think a lot more about the afterlife. I know TJ is in heaven with God, but as a mom, I always want to know what he is doing.

I began researching heaven. It was a drive inside me that caused me to read book after book on heaven and the afterlife. I read many reputable books by great

Christian authors. One, though, that really stood out and meant the most to me was a book by Todd Burpo, *Heaven Is for Real*.

Todd is a pastor in Nebraska who has a very special son named Cody. At three and a half years old, Cody was extremely ill and had to have surgery after his appendix had burst.

He left his body during the surgery and spent time with Jesus in heaven. He did not know that he had done something so special. Over the next couple of months and years, Cody would describe to his astonished parents what heaven was like from a young boy's perspective.

He could describe what each of his parents were doing and where they were in the hospital during his surgery. Over time, he would come to tell them about the people he met in heaven, such as Jesus's cousin, John the Baptist, and his own great-grandfather, whom he had never met or known on earth.

He talked about the angels singing "Jesus loves me!" to him. He talked the most about how much Jesus loves the kids. He said there are so many children in heaven.

I was comforted when Cody said that everyone in heaven has a special job. I could now imagine TJ being a greeter and welcoming people in with excitement, just as he had done at his school and church here on earth.

I really chuckled when he described how everyone had these big wings, because of what TJ said about wanting God to sign his wings. He was so fascinated about how people coveted autographs of Hollywood celebrities and sports stars. In his young mind, he knew we thought of God as way more important than any celebrity!

In *Heaven Is for Real*, when it was time for Cody to leave, he asked Jesus why. Jesus said it was in response to the pleading prayers of Cody's dad; Jesus was answering those prayers!

Wow! Prayer is incredibly important and is so powerful! When we drop to our knees and pray on behalf of our children, parents, and friends, *God listens and responds!*

I know this in a powerful way in my own life. God has been faithful to me throughout the years, but never have I literally felt the power of other people's prayers as during these days and weeks after TJ passed away. The peace and strength that came through our family was like the hand of God wiping the streaming tears off our cheeks with His gentle hand.

Have you ever felt your spirit sensing that someone else is sad even though they have never mentioned that to you? Or have you had a sense of what someone may say to you, and when they said it you, you admitted that you knew exactly what they were going to say?

As parents, you can sense what kind of day your

kids have had when they just come through the door before they have said a word.

I was driving one day, and I asked God, "Why am I not a basket case? Why am I not in a mental institution? I am *not* the emotionally stable type that can handle losing my only son."

I immediately knew. I sensed it with a women's intuition, like when your husband is going to say something or when you know what kind of day your child has had without a word. I've never felt the power of prayer that intensely before.

It was like God spoke and said, "Do you know how many people are praying for you right at this very moment? Hundreds of our Christian brothers and sisters in Christ are empathetically pouring their hearts out for you and your family this very day! They have pleaded with Me for peace in your spirit and for your understanding of the toughest parts of my masterful plan and for wisdom in the saddest part of your journey with Me.

"They asked Me to be a real physical presence in your life and to be an actual true healer of your soul. They have asked Me to search the deepest parts of your hearts and provide for you in ways that only I know about as your loving Father. They have asked to give you a purpose and a destiny that will cause you to rise up in the midst of your suffering and do great things for My glory. How could I, as a loving Father, not grant those requests on your behalf?"

I pondered that for several hours and even in the days to follow. Who are we that people would take our sorrow to God for us daily for weeks and even months, as we would later learn? I could not pray at first. It was not that my faith was wavering, just that I was still too much in shock.

The only prayer that I muttered in this first month was, "God, help me!"

Yet unbeknownst to me, many others were lifting us up and actually carrying our family on the wings of their faithful prayers.

I knew it was not me, but until I sat down and quietly questioned why I was not falling apart and finding myself in a dark abyss of regrets and hopelessness, I realized the *power of those prayers*!

CHAPTER 16

DEALING WITH ANGER

A WEEK AFTER the accident, I called the Ann Arbor police station. Cami and I wanted to see the pictures of the accident. Cami and I are both visual and tactile people. We *needed* to see TJ at the scene, just like we needed to touch his lifeless body and inspect his injuries.

I made an appointment, and Cami and I were ushered into an office the next day. Two officers walked in with a manila envelope. They watched cautiously as Cami and I pored over the photos of the mangled jeep.

We came to the end, and I was frustrated.

"I don't see any pictures of TJ," I stated.

The officers said that there were no pictures of TJ at the scene. Cami and I looked at each other, baffled and disappointed. I argued that there had to be some and that we needed to see them because the hospital never let us say good-bye!

We left with just the photos of the jeep.

So today, two weeks later, Andrea told me that she requested the pictures of the accident be sent to her by e-mail.

Yep! There were all the pictures of TJ at the accident site.

Wow, public protection officers, thanks for not only refusing my rights as a grieving mother and in what would help me heal but lying to me as well.

What I had imagined TJ looking like after the accident was far worse than how he actually looked. His glasses were missing, and his face had dried blood on it, but nothing horrific. I could have wiped it off and kissed him good-bye.

It was helpful to finally see him in the end. It brought a lot of relief and closure. On the other hand, I was furious with the police and the hospital.

My cousin Molly has a doctorate in nursing. She said that the studies show how therapeutic and needful it is for people to say good-bye to their loved ones.

I could totally see myself getting bitter about this. I've been arguing back and forth with myself all day.

"Carrie, you can be angry for a while, but you can't let this take you down. Yes, it's unfair. It's unjust. How could the system let you down! You're definitely not the first or the last to experience unfairness. We live in a human world. Humans make mistakes and let each other down all the time."

Sometimes it helps to talk to myself.

I had to call my mom. She could always talk me down off the edge but, at the same time, empathize with me. She understood my anger. But she let me know that God is still with me. He will comfort me. He will help me get through this.

My mom is the funniest person I know but also one of the wisest and most compassionate.

This was going to take some time and forgiveness. Otherwise, as I've learned the hard way, bitterness affects you badly!

CHAPTER 17

OCTOBER 1, 2010

DEAR TJ

I miss you so much, my wonderful son. I don't know what you know about heaven. I don't know if you are able to see this letter to you. It does not really matter though because I think I need to write this for me.

I think, in a way, you knew you would be leaving us early. In another way, you were sixteen years old and thought you were invincible and could conquer the world. I think you would have been shocked if you knew that God's plan for you was that you would die in a crash on September 12, 2010, on your way to a Sunday evening youth meeting and that would be the last time you saw your friends and family.

I am tormented knowing that your bones were crushed by a tree. I think of you, my broken son, lying there next to a mangled jeep. I wish I could have held you there one last time. Your broken and bleeding, lifeless body in my arms sounds so horrible to anyone else but your mom. But do you remember all the times you and I spent in the ER throughout your life?

Remember how we joked around with the doctors and nurses each time?

You and I always had a way of making any unpleasant experience seem really fun or funny.

I know it meant nothing to you that I was not there when you died. You died instantly and were in the arms of Jesus in the blink of an eye. I did not need to be there for you... I needed to be there for me.

TJ, they wouldn't even let me see you at the hospital that night. Remember how we talked about everything? We had the most open and closely bonded mother-son relationship that most have ever seen.

That is why I need to talk to you about this. You would hug me and then make me smile and laugh really hard all the time.

Remember when you made me laugh so hard and for so long that my migraine actually went away? You actually proved that laughter is the best medicine!

We experienced life together. You helped run the house and take care of the girls in those few years when I was sick and struggling. You grew up to be a handsome tall young man who was so kind and friendly to everyone, made people laugh at you and at themselves, and drew others to you no matter where you were. You had a love and passion for doing the right thing, including serving God through mission trips, and this became infectious to everyone around you.

TJ, you almost didn't make it into this world. Your heart rate dropped, and you went into fetal distress. I had an emergency

C-section, and you were here within minutes. I saw you into this world, and I just wanted to complete my mother role in your life and see you out!

I held you and celebrated you, a gift from God, on February 15, 1994, the happiest day of my young life at that time. I just wish I could have held you on September 12, 2010, and given you back to God on the darkest day of my life!

I know I need to find a way to let it go. There's nothing I can do about it now. The fact is that what's done is done, and I just need to let it go.

God gives and takes away. You would be proud of me, buddy. I never blamed God! I thanked God for the sixteen years he generously gave me with you. God gave me you for only sixteen years and accomplished His will through your life and your death. Your father and I are so honored that God chose us to be your parents.

Thank you for being such an awesome kid. I feel like there is such a hole in my heart without you. I know you are happier than you have ever been. I am so happy for you.

I will not let you down, buddy. I will heal. I will move forward. I will love others without hesitation.

You are up in heaven seeing the whole picture. You want me to do my best for my life after this one. I want to be with you, and I want you to be proud of what I did with life's tragedies.

You inspired me on while you were on earth. I want to be the mom that inspires you as you watch me from heaven.

I love and miss you, my little cowboy.

Chapter 18

JOURNEY THROUGH GRIEF

IT REALLY HELPS me to stick to the facts of losing TJ. It helps me to stay grounded. I just tell myself daily, "Carrie, just stick to the facts."

> Fact: God gave us TJ for exactly sixteen years. He was not taken early or by accident. He did not "miss out" on the things of this life. He was never intended to be married or to have kids of his own. He lived the full life that God intended for him.

> Fact: As a parent, my life's goal is that my children are happy and healthy and safe. TJ is all of that plus a whole lot more in the loving arms of a Heavenly Father. I will always be worried about my girls from time to time as they go through the struggles of this life. But if given the option to come back, I know TJ

would say, "No way!" He is in the safest, happiest, most peaceful place I couldn't even try to imagine.

Fact: No depression, anger, or denial will bring TJ back. Moving forward in joy does not take away from TJ's memory. TJ himself would be disappointed in me if I allowed his death to handicap me and my purpose in life to honor God and to be a cheerleader for others who are in grief.

Fact: It could have been worse. He could have suffered in pain or been on machines until we would have had to make the decision to pull the plug.

He could have been physically or mentally handicapped for the rest of his life. We were actually blessed that he didn't die in a murder or something horrific. If he had to go, I thank God that he was taken quickly and painlessly. There were no drugs or alcohol involved. My heart goes out to the people who have lost loved ones in these ways or have loved ones living in a handicapped situation.

My reality is that I have to deal with the facts of my case to keep myself grounded and sane.

For I know the plans I have for you, says the Lord. They are plans for good and not for disaster, to give you a future and a hope. (Jeremiah 29:11)

This verse was written on the cover of the Bible we gave TJ a couple of years ago. How ironic.

CHAPTER 19

GOOD VERSUS EVIL

Every good and perfect thing comes from above,
from the father of heavenly lights.
—James 1:17a

I WENT TO a Holocaust museum and was so horrified by the pictures and movies I saw of the Jews. I knew about the Holocaust, but the visual images of their constant torture was overwhelming.

I asked God how He could allow this abuse and miserable pain to happen to His chosen people, the Jews. Jesus was a Jew! From what I know about God in my life, he is kind and loving and peaceful and just. I said to God, "This is so opposite of who you are!"

Immediately God stopped my mind from running with that thought. It sounded almost audible when God reminded me that Satan is the prince of this world right now.

Satan even tempted Jesus when Jesus was in the wilderness fasting for forty days. In Matthew 4:8–9, they stood at the top of the mountain, and Satan told Jesus that if He would bow down to him, he would give him all that he could see.

Satan is pure evil and has followers like Hitler and Stalin as well as those who murder and rape, and they carry out his hatred of anyone who loves God.

I read *Ascent from Darkness* by Michael Leehan. He was a Satanist who later became a Christian. He told of his experiences with Satanistic rituals and the spiritual power he experienced as he gave his mind and spirit to Satan. He became angry, cold, bitter, and apathetic toward others. When I read that he fasted and prayed to Satan for the downfall of pastors and other Christians, I really realized where the evil comes from on this earth. He told about this dark spiritual power that he received from Satan. He was constantly filled with anger, depression, and dread. But he was addicted to the power. He told of his desire to kill others and himself. He went into churches for the purpose of causing confusion and pain.

That made me think of the mass shootings in schools and the bombings we see so much of today. I think that kind of rage that harms others and the suicide afterward must be Satanic.

Michael also described the love and peace that he experienced once he turned his life over to God. He convinces his readers that the power of God is far more intense than Satan's.

I have concluded that every good and perfect gift *does* come from God.

Babies, laughter, love, joy, peace, patience, tolerance, mercy, a beautiful day, friendships, music, a kiss, a smile, sacrifices for another person—they all come from God and what He created.

CHAPTER 20

NOT RIGHT OR WRONG— JUST DIFFERENT

TJ'S DEATH OPENED up my heart and mind to so much. I started thinking about what's really important in life. I started thinking about what I get mad over or what upsets me. In the end, these things don't really matter. What you do for others is what you are proud of on your deathbed, in my opinion.

I realized how hard people are on each other. My mom and I were talking about judgmental people this past year. I heard myself ironically judging people for being judgmental. My mom brought up an interesting thought. We all have prejudices against people who don't do things the same way we do or act the same way we do or look the same way as we do. We each think that we make all the right decisions and that our decisions must be right for everyone else.

I had homeschooled TJ, Cassidy, and Cami until TJ was going

into the third grade, Cassie up to second grade, and Cami up to kindergarten.

I enjoyed homeschooling, but due to chronic fatigue syndrome, I just could not do it any longer and keep up. So we sent them to a small Christian school.

They attended there for three years until we moved and just could not afford any of the Christian schools in our new area. So we sent the kids to public school for the first time.

When we sent the kids to Christian school, I did not feel like I had failed as a homeschooling mom. It had become a different season in life.

The same stands true when they went to public school. But something as simple as this can really divide people.

Sometimes we get caught up in the thinking that what *we* do is the right decision all the time and that it is also right for everyone else. But that is not true. I was in a season where God led me to home school. Then in different seasons of our lives, the same God led us in different directions.

This means that God *can* lead one family to home school all their schooling experience while at the same time leading another family to send their kids to public school and others to Christian school. All are doing God's will. My way is not more right than another person's way. It is just different.

God leads Christian parents to train their kids in a certain way that will make them more usable for *His* purposes later in their lives.

We are all called to serve in different ways. Our individual childhoods, trials, successes, and experiences in life all help us to relate to people with similar experiences.

Someone from an abusive past can relate to another person from an abusive past. Someone who has conquered a drug addiction knows how to support a drug addict trying to quit.

Believe it or not, a man covered in tattoos talking about how God has carried him through life is less intimidating to some people than a man in a suit carrying a Bible.

We need to stop judging and comparing ourselves to each other. What I am called to do with my gifts and talents can be drastically different from my Christian brothers and sisters.

The only thing I can take with me to heaven is relationships. I can't take my house or clothes or any materials that I've worked hard to buy.

Spending time with others has become my number one priority. Telling people about my son and his love and respect for God is so healing for me.

I also want everyone to go to heaven with me when I die. I know TJ would want me to tell others about Jesus's sacrifice for us and that we *can* know for sure that we will go to heaven when we die. Believing in Jesus and having a relationship with Him is not only for our eternal security, but it makes life worth more than in just serving ourselves.

CHAPTER 21

DREAMS

I HAVE HAD a lot of vivid dreams since TJ's death. I can usually remember at least one dream, and then bits and pieces of others throughout the day come back to me.

On June 7 at 8:30 a.m., I awoke so suddenly and was amazed at what had just occurred in my dreamworld.

In my dream, my husband and I and our two teenage girls had moved to a new house. When it got dark, things began to come out of the woodwork. Scary faces, bugs, and things scampering past my feet were making this new house frightening.

In this dream, I went to wake Trent up to tell him what was happening, and when he sat up, he was wearing a freaky tribal mask.

I took it off him, and our family huddled together on the bed. Suddenly, part of the paneling on the wall came loose, and we knew something horrifying was about to emerge.

Let's step away from the dream for a minute. I need to give an explanation about what I did next in my dream. The New Testament cites many times when Jesus, and later his disciples, cast demons out of possessed people.

The one thing that has resonated with me is how much demons hate hearing the name of Jesus. People throughout history have tried many ways to get rid of demons and evil spirits. The one thing that has been continually successful is the name of Jesus.

Back to my dream: we were all terrified, watching something about to come out of the wall.

Then I instinctively called out, "Jesus! Help me!"

Instantly I woke up to hear myself whisper, "Jesus, help me." Wow. I shouted that and actually said that loud enough to wake myself up in my dream, but I woke up to myself whispering it.

I realized that calling out Jesus's name was powerful enough to rescue me from my dreamworld.

I totally get that this seems crazy to a lot of people. I would feel the same way if I wasn't the one experiencing these things. I have just been so aware of this spirit world that's beyond us.

Why do we make movies about good versus evil? Why do we gravitate toward the ones where good wins over evil? How did that come from evolution, that we recognize the ethics and morality of light versus darkness?

In the book *Chicken Soup for the Christian Soul*, there is a story called "Prayer Is the Key."

It tells of a story of a medic who was a missionary in Africa. Sometimes he needed to travel by bicycle to other cities for supplies.

One day, he saw two men fighting. He treated one of the men

for personal injuries, and everything was fine. A couple of weeks later, the medic came by his place again and ran into the same man he had treated.

The man told him how he and his friends had followed the medic to his campsite and had planned to rob and kill him. But they didn't do it because he was surrounded by twenty-six armed guards.

Several months later, the medic was speaking at one of his supporting churches about the incident. He was surprised to find out that while it was at night when this happened, it was morning in the United States and twenty-six men had been praying for him.

Again, that's coincidence? How do we humans deny that there's a spirit world?

CHAPTER 22

A LETTER TO TJ

MARCH 27, 2011

Where are you? It is spring now. This was the time when you and your dad would sit on the back porch swing and watch the sun go down for an hour or so. You and your dad would sit out back day after day, talking and watching the sunsets in the warm weather. You guys had so many man-to-man talks about philosophy, theology, little things, and just life itself. I would clean up the kitchen and watch out the back window at you boys talking and working out your manly ways.

Winter is over now, both physically and emotionally. We went through the cold, hard, harsh, dark days of winter. Spring is upon us, and the sun and light are more frequent now. We made it through those darkest of days. I feel spring budding in my heart and see spring blooming in my yard. I look for you, yet you're still not there. With the new season comes the memory of last season with you.

How can it be a lighter season—with new budding plants, flowers, and new babies—without you?

Our pain is less than it was in the winter. Emotionally we are moving on; we are allowing the new growth to move in. We are welcoming it in many ways. It is a relief from the dark, cold winter. But how can we allow the warmer, happier season to soothe us without you welcoming it in with us?

You died in September. The fall of our weather and the "fall" of our emotional condition coincided. This winter in Michigan was cold, hard, dismal, sobering, and empty. I wanted to hibernate in a dark cave like a mama bear.

Our family had to endure the bitter cold both physically and emotionally in order to experience spring and new growth.

I love and miss you, TJ!

Love,
Mom

CHAPTER 23

HELL

I FELT MY senses heightened about the spiritual realm in regard to God, but then I wondered about the opposite side. I pursued an investigation into the "dark side."

I read the book *23 Minutes in Hell* by Bill Weise. He is a Christian whom God brought to hell so he could come back and write a book to warn us of what would come if we didn't embrace Jesus.

His description of hell is consistent with the Bible's. Bill woke up in hell to the sight of terrifying demons with scales like fish. They are huge creatures and very dark. He experienced dryness like a desert and felt so thirsty. He felt hopelessness and dread at the reality that this was eternity. He mourned as he knew that he would never see his family and friends again.

You hear of people saying that they don't care about going to hell because they'll be there with friends or family. But Bill told of all the lonely people there in places where they were isolated from everyone, especially friends and family. All you could see were demons. All you could hear were screams and wailing. He describes the reality of you knowing that this hopelessness was how you will spend eternity alone.

There was a portal from hell to heaven where Jesus brought Bill out. He told Bill that he needed him to experience what he did so he could write a book warning others. Jesus told him that it hurt him deeply when he saw people going to hell.

CHAPTER 24

GRANDMA PROCTOR

MY MATERNAL GREAT-GRANDMOTHER lived to 104 years old. She believed that the reason for her longevity was due to faith and humor. She had so much faith in God and prayed all day long every day. It obviously didn't hurt her, and I would venture to agree that it might have served her well!

In her last days, she seemed to have a glimpse into the heaven she was about to enter.

My mom was with her on one of these last nights on earth. Grandma was blind but seemed to see something my mom could not. Grandma was describing what she saw in heaven. She exclaimed, "Oh, this little boy is up here without his parents." She reached out to hug him.

My mom, recognizing Grandma being somewhere else, stepped up to embrace her as the little boy. My mom said that Grandma's hug was so warm and so tight and so long!

This happened ten years before TJ died. But now I feel so

comforted that Grandma Proctor is hugging my boy and taking good care of him until I get there! Thank you, God, for that!

Grandma died on September 12, 2000. It was two months short of her 105th birthday. Exactly ten years to the day when TJ died. I feel like Grandma and TJ were/are spiritually connected.

I wonder sometimes if God communicates with us through numbers. TJ died when he was sixteen years old. His funeral was on September 16. When Trent and I were looking at cemetery plots, I wanted one in the old part of the cemetery by the lake because I rode my bike through there all the time. It's a beautiful hilly cemetery, and it was my place of quiet reflection. They only had one plot left there. It was plot number 16.

CHAPTER 25

END OF 2011

THEY SAY THAT time heals all wounds. Time does have a way of moving, and of moving us.

Lydia has gone through an event you would never want anyone you love to have to go through. She has physically had to endure great pain and work to regain what she had. She continues to see a chiropractor weekly to help keep her back and hips adjusted. She also has some short-term memory issues that are a result of the damage her brain endured. Emotionally, she has gone through the loss of her first love—a complete loss, not just heartbreak. Spiritually, she has dealt with doubts and whys.

I continue to talk to Carrie almost on a daily basis. We meet with each other for dinner and reminiscing every month. We talk, we cry, and best of all, we laugh. She means the world to me. I still always take her calls!

CHAPTER 26

WILSECKS

ANDREA AND I have grown very close since the accident. I love her so much, and we have an everlasting friendship. We have spoken at churches together a couple of times. We look forward to our dinners out every month.

Roy is in his first year of college now. My whole extended family has adopted the Wilseck kids as our own. Liz has Roy come over to her house on his breaks. He plays with her kids and has talks with Liz like TJ did. He even goes to the movies with Liz while the kids are in school, like TJ enjoyed doing.

Liz's kids love Roy like their cousin. I think it's good for both Liz and Roy. Roy doesn't do it out of obligation because TJ isn't here. I think he does it for therapy and for TJ.

Cami and Josiah have gotten to be close friends. They text each other from time to time.

I will always have a warm spot in my heart for Lydia. We texted each other a lot during the first year. I pray for her a lot and ask God to heal her heart. I will always have a love for the "little girl" whom my son loved almost as much as his car!

She wrote a beautiful story I'd like to share:

FEBRUARY 14, 2011

We fall in love so easily, with a good book, a TV show, or even a slice of pizza. Love is taken for granted every day. True love, however, is like a diamond in the rough. It is nearly impossible to find, but once you discover love, you better hold on to it. On April 23, 2010, a girl met her true love. The love was pure and beautiful, something that relationships these days lack. The boy and girl fit so well together, and when they started dating, no one could've guessed how long their relationship would last. Somehow, everything worked perfectly for the couple, and they enjoyed every second of the relationship.

The beginning of the relationship was laughter. From the first day they met to the last second they were together, the couple laughed. Both of them had the same unique and interesting humor; they enjoyed making fun of people. The times they were together, there was constant joking and laughter. It was as if God had set it up perfectly: the time, the ridiculous person, and the random place to make the couple take one look, turn to each other, and burst out laughing. This humor brought the couple so close together and made the relationship fun and pure.

By the middle of this relationship, the two decided they wanted to get to know the other's family. The boy's mom was always happy and smiling, much like the girl's. Soon, the teens' moms became close. This, of course, made it even easier for the two to be together. The more time the couple spent with each other's families, the more they got to know each other. The bond was deep inside the two; it was as if they had grown up together.

One day, as the couple was sitting together, eating bagels, the boy asked about death. "Would you be upset if I died?" he asked.

"Of course I would! I would cry and—"

"No, seriously, take a minute and think about it," he told her. She paused for a minute and, although she knew her answer already, thought. "I would be devastated," she started. "Nothing would ever be the same. If you died, I wouldn't be happy until I was with you again." The boy made her promise to never hurt herself because of him. He brought up death quite often in their conversations, but the girl never thought anything of it.

Then the day came: the couple had just finished a long day at school and were finally going home. "Tell me that you love me," said the boy

"I love you, baby," the girl replied. They got in the car and drove off. When the girl woke up, she was in a bed. She found out that the love of her life was gone forever. There was a steady pain in her heart, and all she could think was *they're wrong.* She waited for him to come bouncing in with his gorgeous smile and those amazing eyes shining. She finally realized that he wasn't coming back; a love so deep was ripped to shreds, leaving only one broken heart as proof. And although it killed her inside, the girl knew that she had to be strong, for him. Their love could never be replaced or compared with anything. And she only hopes to find something so wonderful again.

CONCLUSION

IT'S JANUARY 2012. I have been writing this book for a year and a half. I think about my experiences during this time. This is what I came away with.

I don't know what or where I would be without prayer. I have met many who have lost loved ones, especially children. Many are not doing well years later.

I think, *Why is that not me? Why have I moved on with laughter, peace, joy, and so much more love?*

When I compare my experience to others, not much is different except for one thing. Prayer. From the hour that TJ died, the news took off on Facebook, phone calls, texts, and e-mails. It was a wildfire of horror and shock to family, friends, students, and even strangers. The cards and messages started flowing in, even from some people I didn't know but were devastated by our story.

Almost all the messages we received promised prayers on our behalf. We were on about fifty church prayer lists around the country and even other countries, and that's just the ones I know about. There were thousands of people praying for us!

Two months ago, I was feeling depressed and angry at nothing in particular. I felt a heaviness in my chest and a darkness in my spirit. I decided to go to the gym and work it out of me. My prayers were inhibited for some reason. After two hours on the treadmill, I decided to text my mom.

In my family, we have our own prayer chain. If someone has a prayer request, we text our mom, Grandma, or Aunt Kay, and they forward it to the other family members who have volunteered to be prayer warriors.

I texted my mom and said that I was struggling. I felt depression, anger, rage, and a darkness over me.

I was walking on the treadmill at the same pace I had been at for the last twenty minutes. I looked at my heart rate. It was 155 beats per minute.

It had been about three minutes since I had sent Mom the message. All of a sudden, I felt a peace wash through me like a warm shower. I had been staring at the heartbeat number and watched it drop to 130 in 5 seconds. I felt lighter and happier. My spirit leaped within me, and I thought, *Wow, God! That was amazing!*

I felt like I had just witnessed prayer at work, not just spiritually but physically! It made me think of when TJ made me laugh so hard my headache disappeared. The Bible says that laughter is the best medicine, and it was physically proven.

Prayer is so powerful. We don't utilize it enough. I've seen so many times that prayer has changed my life, whether I was the one praying for someone else or the recipient.

Faith has been my best friend these past sixteen months. Yes, it took me sixteen months to write this, and no, I didn't intend that.

Sometimes I have to say no to my kids or let painful, natural consequences run their course to teach them that it's because I love them and want them to learn to make good choices. Sometimes I have to watch them hurt because I know it's how you learn to do life. I don't do things on purpose to hurt them, and I come beside them to guide and comfort them while they're learning.

A baby learns to walk by falling, sometimes getting hurt. We comfort them.

Sometimes, spiritually and emotionally, we are learning to walk. God doesn't push us down. But he's always there to comfort us. We learn about life through natural consequences, mistakes, good and bad choices, age, etc. But if we need help and cry out to God, he will guide us. If my kids want to make wrong choices, they'll learn the hard way. But if they ask me to help them, I would in a heartbeat.

I think people don't feel like God helps them because they don't ask. We have free will, and if we want to do life our way, God is hands-off. He helps us when we cry out to him.

If one of my kids needs something, I'll hear them out. But if all the siblings come to me on behalf of another, the urgency and the concern they have for each other moves me greater. That's my picture of prayer.

I have had faith that God has been comforting me and made TJ's death as merciful as possible. The way TJ died, the multitudes of people that were there for us, the family and community support, and the lessons God lovingly taught me throughout this experience.

Sixteen months later, I am a better wife and mom. I am a more loving friend, daughter, granddaughter, and niece. I am a more friendly stranger. I am more thankful, gracious, and sincere. I am more.

SPECIAL THANK YOU

I would like to thank those who met us and prayed with us at the hospital that night. That room of people will be forever imprinted in my mind as such an intimate group: Both sets of my parents; Liz and Thomas; our pastor, Darril Holden; youth pastor Phil Bell; my mom's pastor, Jim Mascow; John, Nancy, and Colin Slaughter; Matt and Sarah Cotterman; Carrie Townley; and my cousin Kelsey were our support and prayer team that night. I look back at that scene, and it was so sad but so comforting.

FAMILY

We would like to thank our family, who have supported us before, during, and after the accident. Trent had family come in from all over the country. His mom and sister, Stacy, kept up my kitchen during this time. They also kept Trent fed and hydrated.

My mom and sister, Liz, were my decision makers. They helped me do things that I couldn't do and did things for me. My brother, Andy, came up from Florida and was a source of strength.

My dad and stepmom and Trent's dad and stepmom also brought support.

My twin cousins, Polly and Molly, set up the TJ Mission Fund for donations to help kids who normally couldn't afford these trips. Last summer our church was able to take over seventy kids and leaders to Tennessee to help poor people fix up their houses. Our church had only taken about twenty people at the most on mission's trips in the past.

My cousin Betsy sang for the funeral. I appreciated her strength during a tough situation.

FRIENDS

My friends Sarah Cotterman and Julie Hardesty made sure I was eating, drinking, and getting bathroom breaks during the viewing and funeral. My friend Lauren Chandler dropped off a couple of cases of water in bottles, which were a really big help.

We had so many friends bringing us food, helpful books, and anything we needed. Unfortunately, there are too many too name.

CHURCH

The church had meals coming to our house every other day for a couple of weeks. We had the funeral at the church, and they also fixed and served the dinner after.

PRAYER WARRIORS

Thank you to you who know who you are!